50 Italian Appetizer Recipes for Home

By: Kelly Johnson

Table of Contents

- Bruschetta with Tomato and Basil
- Caprese Salad Skewers
- Arancini (Stuffed Rice Balls)
- Antipasto Platter with Cured Meats and Cheeses
- Fried Calamari with Marinara Sauce
- Stuffed Mushrooms with Cheese and Herbs
- Prosciutto-Wrapped Asparagus
- Mozzarella Sticks with Marinara Dipping Sauce
- Focaccia Bread with Olive Oil and Balsamic Vinegar
- Grilled Polenta Bites with Pesto
- Panzanella (Tuscan Bread Salad) Skewers
- Spinach and Ricotta Stuffed Shells
- Baked Eggplant Parmesan Bites
- Italian Sausage and Pepper Skewers
- Garlic Shrimp Bruschetta
- Tomato and Mozzarella Tartlets
- Mini Meatball Sliders
- Ricotta and Spinach Stuffed Mushrooms
- Crostini with Goat Cheese and Roasted Red Peppers
- Polenta Crostini with Gorgonzola and Honey
- Zucchini Fritters with Garlic Aioli
- Caprese Stuffed Avocado
- Italian Wedding Soup Shooters
- Mini Margherita Pizzas
- Grilled Artichoke Hearts with Lemon Garlic Aioli
- Olive Tapenade Crostini
- Baked Zucchini Parmesan Chips
- Ricotta and Tomato Bruschetta
- Grilled Prosciutto-Wrapped Figs
- Parmesan and Herb Puff Pastry Twists
- Fried Ravioli with Marinara Sauce
- Italian Stuffed Bell Peppers
- Roasted Red Pepper and Feta Bruschetta
- Caprese Skewers with Balsamic Glaze
- Mushroom and Fontina Arancini

- Caponata Crostini
- Sausage and Ricotta Stuffed Mushrooms
- Pesto Palmiers
- Tomato Basil Bruschetta Cups
- Italian Stuffed Artichokes
- Sun-Dried Tomato and Olive Tapenade
- Pesto and Sun-Dried Tomato Pinwheels
- Ricotta and Spinach Stuffed Pasta Shells
- Italian Cheese Fondue with Bread Cubes
- Mini Calzones with Marinara Dipping Sauce
- Grilled Prosciutto-Wrapped Shrimp
- Italian Herb and Cheese Pull-Apart Bread
- Sautéed Garlic Butter Shrimp
- Mediterranean Stuffed Mini Peppers
- Fried Mozzarella and Tomato Bites

Bruschetta with Tomato and Basil

Ingredients:

- 4-5 ripe tomatoes, diced
- 1/4 cup fresh basil leaves, chopped
- 2 cloves garlic, minced
- 2 tablespoons extra virgin olive oil
- 1 tablespoon balsamic vinegar
- Salt and pepper to taste
- 1 baguette, sliced into 1/2-inch thick slices
- Olive oil for brushing

Instructions:

1. Preheat your oven to 375°F (190°C).
2. In a mixing bowl, combine the diced tomatoes, chopped basil, minced garlic, extra virgin olive oil, balsamic vinegar, salt, and pepper. Mix well to combine all the ingredients. Set aside to marinate while you prepare the bread.
3. Place the baguette slices on a baking sheet in a single layer. Lightly brush each slice with olive oil on both sides.
4. Bake the bread slices in the preheated oven for about 5-7 minutes, or until they are lightly toasted and golden brown. Keep an eye on them to prevent burning.
5. Once the bread is toasted, remove it from the oven and let it cool slightly.
6. Once cooled, spoon the tomato and basil mixture generously onto each toasted bread slice.
7. Arrange the bruschetta on a serving platter and serve immediately, while the bread is still warm.

Enjoy your delicious Bruschetta with Tomato and Basil as a flavorful appetizer or snack!

Caprese Salad Skewers

Ingredients:

- Fresh mozzarella balls (bocconcini), drained
- Cherry tomatoes
- Fresh basil leaves
- Balsamic glaze
- Bamboo skewers

Instructions:

1. Start by assembling your skewers. Thread a cherry tomato onto a skewer, followed by a fresh basil leaf folded in half, then a mozzarella ball, and finally another cherry tomato. Repeat this pattern until the skewer is filled, leaving a little space at the end for easy handling.
2. Continue assembling skewers until you have made enough for your desired serving size.
3. Once all the skewers are assembled, arrange them on a serving platter.
4. Just before serving, drizzle the skewers with balsamic glaze for a sweet and tangy finish.
5. Serve the Caprese Salad Skewers immediately as a delightful appetizer or hors d'oeuvre at your next gathering.

These skewers are not only delicious but also provide a beautiful presentation, making them perfect for parties, potlucks, or any occasion where you want to impress your guests with a tasty and elegant dish. Enjoy!

Arancini (Stuffed Rice Balls)

Ingredients:

- 2 cups Arborio rice
- 4 cups chicken or vegetable broth
- 1/2 cup grated Parmesan cheese
- 1/4 cup chopped fresh parsley
- Salt and pepper to taste
- 1 cup breadcrumbs
- 2 eggs, beaten
- Mozzarella cheese, cut into small cubes
- Marinara sauce for serving
- Vegetable oil for frying

Instructions:

1. In a large saucepan, bring the chicken or vegetable broth to a simmer over medium heat.
2. Add the Arborio rice to the broth and cook, stirring occasionally, until the rice is tender and the liquid is absorbed, about 18-20 minutes.
3. Once the rice is cooked, remove it from the heat and let it cool slightly.
4. Stir in the grated Parmesan cheese, chopped parsley, salt, and pepper until well combined. Allow the mixture to cool completely.
5. Once the rice mixture has cooled, take a small handful of the mixture and flatten it in the palm of your hand. Place a cube of mozzarella cheese in the center and shape the rice mixture into a ball around the cheese, making sure it is tightly packed.
6. Repeat this process with the remaining rice mixture and mozzarella cheese cubes until you have used all the rice.
7. In one shallow bowl, place the beaten eggs. In another shallow bowl, place the breadcrumbs.
8. Dip each rice ball into the beaten eggs, then roll it in the breadcrumbs until evenly coated. Set the coated rice balls aside on a plate.
9. In a large skillet or deep fryer, heat vegetable oil to 350°F (175°C).
10. Carefully place a few rice balls into the hot oil and fry until golden brown and crispy, about 3-4 minutes. Remove the fried arancini from the oil and drain on a paper towel-lined plate.

11. Repeat the frying process with the remaining rice balls, working in batches as needed.
12. Serve the arancini hot with marinara sauce for dipping.

These delicious stuffed rice balls are crispy on the outside, creamy and cheesy on the inside, and make for a perfect appetizer or snack for any occasion. Enjoy!

Antipasto Platter with Cured Meats and Cheeses

Ingredients:

- Assorted cured meats (such as prosciutto, salami, coppa, or soppressata)
- Assorted cheeses (such as mozzarella, provolone, Parmesan, or aged cheddar)
- Olives (such as Kalamata, green, or Castelvetrano)
- Marinated vegetables (such as artichoke hearts, roasted red peppers, or sun-dried tomatoes)
- Pickles (such as gherkins or cornichons)
- Nuts (such as almonds, walnuts, or pistachios)
- Fresh fruit (such as grapes, figs, or sliced apples)
- Breadsticks or crackers
- Extra virgin olive oil and balsamic vinegar for drizzling
- Fresh herbs for garnish (such as basil, thyme, or rosemary)

Instructions:

1. Start by selecting a large platter or wooden board to arrange your antipasto ingredients.
2. Arrange the cured meats on the platter, folding or rolling them for a visually appealing presentation.
3. Next, arrange the assorted cheeses around the cured meats. You can slice or cube the cheeses for easy serving.
4. Fill in the gaps on the platter with olives, marinated vegetables, pickles, and nuts.
5. Add fresh fruit to the platter, scattering it around for pops of color and flavor.
6. Arrange breadsticks or crackers on the platter for serving alongside the meats and cheeses.
7. Drizzle extra virgin olive oil and balsamic vinegar over the cheeses and vegetables for added flavor.
8. Garnish the platter with fresh herbs for a finishing touch.
9. Serve the antipasto platter as a starter or appetizer before a meal, or as a standalone dish for entertaining guests.

This antipasto platter is not only delicious but also offers a variety of flavors and textures that will satisfy everyone's palate. Enjoy!

Fried Calamari with Marinara Sauce

Ingredients:

For the fried calamari:

- 1 pound (450g) squid (calamari), cleaned and sliced into rings
- 1 cup all-purpose flour
- 1 teaspoon salt
- 1/2 teaspoon black pepper
- 1/2 teaspoon garlic powder
- 1/2 teaspoon paprika
- Vegetable oil, for frying

For the marinara sauce:

- 2 tablespoons olive oil
- 2 cloves garlic, minced
- 1 can (14 ounces) crushed tomatoes
- 1 teaspoon dried oregano
- 1 teaspoon dried basil
- Salt and pepper to taste
- Pinch of red pepper flakes (optional)
- Fresh parsley, chopped (for garnish)

Instructions:

1. Start by preparing the marinara sauce. Heat the olive oil in a saucepan over medium heat. Add the minced garlic and sauté for 1-2 minutes until fragrant.
2. Pour in the crushed tomatoes and add the dried oregano, dried basil, salt, pepper, and red pepper flakes (if using). Stir to combine.
3. Bring the sauce to a simmer and let it cook for about 10-15 minutes, stirring occasionally, until it thickens slightly. Taste and adjust seasoning if needed. Remove from heat and set aside.
4. In a shallow bowl, combine the all-purpose flour, salt, black pepper, garlic powder, and paprika. Mix well.
5. Heat vegetable oil in a deep fryer or large pot to 350°F (175°C).
6. Dip the calamari rings into the seasoned flour mixture, shaking off any excess.

7. Carefully place the coated calamari rings into the hot oil, working in batches to avoid overcrowding the pot. Fry for about 2-3 minutes, or until golden brown and crispy.
8. Use a slotted spoon to remove the fried calamari from the oil and transfer them to a plate lined with paper towels to drain any excess oil.
9. Sprinkle the fried calamari with a little salt while they are still hot.
10. Serve the fried calamari immediately with the marinara sauce on the side for dipping.
11. Garnish with chopped fresh parsley for added flavor and presentation.

Enjoy your crispy fried calamari with marinara sauce as a delicious appetizer or snack!

Stuffed Mushrooms with Cheese and Herbs

Ingredients:

- 12 large mushrooms, cleaned with stems removed
- 1 tablespoon olive oil
- 2 cloves garlic, minced
- 1/4 cup breadcrumbs
- 1/4 cup grated Parmesan cheese
- 1/4 cup shredded mozzarella cheese
- 2 tablespoons chopped fresh parsley
- Salt and pepper to taste

Instructions:

1. Preheat your oven to 375°F (190°C). Line a baking sheet with parchment paper or lightly grease it with olive oil.
2. In a skillet, heat the olive oil over medium heat. Add the minced garlic and sauté for 1-2 minutes until fragrant.
3. Chop the mushroom stems finely and add them to the skillet. Cook for another 2-3 minutes until the mushroom stems are softened.
4. Remove the skillet from heat and transfer the cooked mushroom stems and garlic to a mixing bowl.
5. To the mixing bowl, add the breadcrumbs, grated Parmesan cheese, shredded mozzarella cheese, chopped fresh parsley, salt, and pepper. Mix well to combine all the ingredients.
6. Take each mushroom cap and fill it with the prepared stuffing mixture, pressing gently to pack it in.
7. Place the stuffed mushrooms on the prepared baking sheet.
8. Bake in the preheated oven for 18-20 minutes, or until the mushrooms are tender and the filling is golden brown and bubbly.
9. Once done, remove the stuffed mushrooms from the oven and let them cool for a few minutes before serving.
10. Serve the stuffed mushrooms warm as an appetizer or side dish. Enjoy!

These stuffed mushrooms are flavorful, cheesy, and packed with delicious herbs, making them a crowd-pleasing dish for any occasion.

Prosciutto-Wrapped Asparagus

Ingredients:

- 1 bunch of asparagus spears, tough ends trimmed
- 6-8 slices of prosciutto
- Olive oil, for drizzling
- Salt and pepper to taste
- Balsamic glaze (optional), for serving

Instructions:

1. Preheat your oven to 400°F (200°C). Line a baking sheet with parchment paper or aluminum foil for easy cleanup.
2. Take each asparagus spear and wrap it with a slice of prosciutto, starting from the bottom and spiraling upwards. You can use half a slice of prosciutto if the spears are thin.
3. Place the prosciutto-wrapped asparagus spears on the prepared baking sheet in a single layer.
4. Drizzle the asparagus with olive oil and season with salt and pepper to taste. You can also omit the salt if your prosciutto is particularly salty.
5. Roast the prosciutto-wrapped asparagus in the preheated oven for 10-12 minutes, or until the asparagus is tender and the prosciutto is crispy.
6. Once done, remove the baking sheet from the oven and let the asparagus cool slightly.
7. Transfer the prosciutto-wrapped asparagus to a serving platter and drizzle with balsamic glaze, if desired, for an extra burst of flavor.
8. Serve the prosciutto-wrapped asparagus as a delicious appetizer or side dish. Enjoy!

This dish is simple to make yet elegant and flavorful, making it perfect for entertaining or as a special treat for yourself.

Mozzarella Sticks with Marinara Dipping Sauce

Ingredients:

For the mozzarella sticks:

- 12 sticks of mozzarella cheese, cut into rectangles or sticks
- 1 cup all-purpose flour
- 2 large eggs, beaten
- 1 cup breadcrumbs
- 1 teaspoon dried Italian herbs (optional)
- 1/2 teaspoon garlic powder (optional)
- Salt and pepper to taste
- Vegetable oil, for frying

For the marinara dipping sauce:

- 1 tablespoon olive oil
- 2 cloves garlic, minced
- 1 can (14 ounces) crushed tomatoes
- 1 teaspoon dried oregano
- 1 teaspoon dried basil
- Salt and pepper to taste
- Pinch of red pepper flakes (optional)
- Fresh basil leaves, chopped (for garnish)

Instructions:

1. Prepare the mozzarella sticks by cutting the mozzarella cheese into rectangles or sticks, about 1/2 inch thick.
2. Set up a breading station with three shallow bowls. Place the flour in the first bowl, beaten eggs in the second bowl, and breadcrumbs mixed with dried Italian herbs, garlic powder, salt, and pepper in the third bowl.
3. Dredge each mozzarella stick in the flour, shaking off any excess. Then dip it into the beaten eggs, allowing any excess to drip off. Finally, coat it in the breadcrumbs mixture, pressing gently to adhere.
4. Place the breaded mozzarella sticks on a baking sheet lined with parchment paper and freeze them for about 30 minutes to help them firm up.
5. While the mozzarella sticks are chilling, prepare the marinara dipping sauce. Heat olive oil in a saucepan over medium heat. Add minced garlic and sauté for 1-2 minutes until fragrant.

6. Pour in the crushed tomatoes and add dried oregano, dried basil, salt, pepper, and red pepper flakes (if using). Stir to combine.
7. Bring the sauce to a simmer and let it cook for about 10-15 minutes, stirring occasionally, until it thickens slightly. Taste and adjust seasoning if needed. Remove from heat and set aside.
8. Heat vegetable oil in a deep fryer or large pot to 350°F (175°C). Carefully fry the mozzarella sticks in batches for about 2-3 minutes, or until golden brown and crispy.
9. Use a slotted spoon to remove the fried mozzarella sticks from the oil and transfer them to a plate lined with paper towels to drain any excess oil.
10. Sprinkle the fried mozzarella sticks with a little salt while they are still hot.
11. Serve the mozzarella sticks immediately with the marinara dipping sauce on the side for dipping.
12. Garnish with chopped fresh basil leaves for added flavor and presentation.

Enjoy your homemade mozzarella sticks with marinara dipping sauce as a delicious appetizer or snack!

Focaccia Bread with Olive Oil and Balsamic Vinegar

Ingredients:

For the focaccia bread:

- 1 package (2 1/4 teaspoons) active dry yeast
- 1 1/2 cups warm water (about 110°F/45°C)
- 1 tablespoon granulated sugar
- 4 cups all-purpose flour
- 1 teaspoon salt
- 1/4 cup extra virgin olive oil, plus more for drizzling
- Coarse sea salt, for sprinkling
- Fresh rosemary leaves, for garnish (optional)

For serving:

- Extra virgin olive oil
- Balsamic vinegar

Instructions:

1. In a large mixing bowl, combine the warm water, granulated sugar, and active dry yeast. Let it sit for about 5-10 minutes, or until the yeast is frothy and activated.
2. Add the flour, salt, and 1/4 cup of olive oil to the bowl with the yeast mixture. Stir until a shaggy dough forms.
3. Turn the dough out onto a floured surface and knead it for about 5-7 minutes, or until it becomes smooth and elastic.
4. Place the kneaded dough in a lightly greased bowl, cover it with a clean kitchen towel or plastic wrap, and let it rise in a warm, draft-free place for about 1-1.5 hours, or until it doubles in size.
5. Preheat your oven to 400°F (200°C). Grease a baking sheet or line it with parchment paper.
6. Punch down the risen dough and transfer it to the prepared baking sheet. Press the dough out into a rectangle or oval shape, about 1/2 inch thick.
7. Use your fingertips to make indentations all over the surface of the dough. Drizzle the top of the dough with olive oil and sprinkle with coarse sea salt. If desired, scatter fresh rosemary leaves over the top of the dough for added flavor.
8. Bake the focaccia bread in the preheated oven for 20-25 minutes, or until it is golden brown and cooked through.

9. Once done, remove the focaccia bread from the oven and let it cool slightly on a wire rack.
10. To serve, slice the focaccia bread into pieces and serve warm or at room temperature. Drizzle with extra virgin olive oil and balsamic vinegar for dipping.
11. Enjoy your homemade focaccia bread with olive oil and balsamic vinegar as a delicious appetizer or side dish!

This focaccia bread is soft, fluffy, and infused with the flavors of olive oil and balsamic vinegar, making it the perfect accompaniment to any meal.

Grilled Polenta Bites with Pesto

Ingredients:

For the polenta:

- 1 cup polenta or cornmeal
- 4 cups water or vegetable broth
- 1 teaspoon salt
- 1/2 cup grated Parmesan cheese
- 2 tablespoons butter or olive oil

For the pesto:

- 2 cups fresh basil leaves, packed
- 1/2 cup grated Parmesan cheese
- 1/4 cup pine nuts or walnuts
- 2 cloves garlic
- 1/2 cup extra virgin olive oil
- Salt and pepper to taste

Instructions:

1. Prepare the polenta: In a large saucepan, bring the water or vegetable broth to a boil. Gradually whisk in the polenta or cornmeal, stirring constantly to prevent lumps from forming.
2. Reduce the heat to low and continue to cook the polenta, stirring frequently, until it is thick and creamy, about 15-20 minutes. Add more water or broth if necessary to achieve the desired consistency.
3. Once the polenta is cooked, remove it from the heat and stir in the grated Parmesan cheese and butter or olive oil until melted and well combined. Season with salt to taste.
4. Pour the cooked polenta into a greased baking dish or sheet pan, spreading it out evenly to a thickness of about 1/2 inch. Smooth the top with a spatula.
5. Allow the polenta to cool and set in the refrigerator for at least 1 hour, or until firm.
6. Meanwhile, prepare the pesto: In a food processor or blender, combine the basil leaves, grated Parmesan cheese, pine nuts or walnuts, and garlic. Pulse until finely chopped.
7. With the food processor running, slowly drizzle in the extra virgin olive oil until the pesto reaches a smooth and creamy consistency. Season with salt and pepper to taste.
8. Preheat your grill or grill pan to medium-high heat. Cut the chilled polenta into bite-sized squares or rectangles.
9. Lightly brush the polenta bites with olive oil and grill them for 3-4 minutes per side, or until golden brown and slightly crispy.

10. Remove the grilled polenta bites from the grill and transfer them to a serving platter. Top each bite with a dollop of pesto.
11. Serve the grilled polenta bites with pesto immediately as a delicious appetizer or side dish.

These grilled polenta bites with pesto are flavorful, satisfying, and sure to be a hit at your next gathering or party! Enjoy!

Panzanella (Tuscan Bread Salad) Skewers

Ingredients:

For the skewers:

- Cherry tomatoes
- Cubed bread (such as ciabatta or sourdough)
- Cucumber, cut into chunks
- Red onion, cut into chunks
- Fresh basil leaves
- Balsamic glaze (optional), for drizzling

For the dressing:

- 1/4 cup extra virgin olive oil
- 2 tablespoons balsamic vinegar
- 1 clove garlic, minced
- Salt and pepper to taste

Instructions:

1. Preheat your grill or grill pan to medium-high heat.
2. Assemble the skewers by threading cherry tomatoes, cubed bread, cucumber chunks, red onion chunks, and fresh basil leaves onto skewers, alternating the ingredients as desired.
3. In a small bowl, whisk together the extra virgin olive oil, balsamic vinegar, minced garlic, salt, and pepper to make the dressing.
4. Brush the assembled skewers with some of the dressing, reserving the rest for serving.
5. Grill the skewers on the preheated grill for 2-3 minutes per side, or until the bread is lightly toasted and the vegetables are slightly charred.
6. Once grilled, remove the skewers from the grill and transfer them to a serving platter.
7. Drizzle the grilled skewers with the remaining dressing and balsamic glaze, if using.
8. Serve the Panzanella skewers immediately as a delicious appetizer or side dish.

These Panzanella skewers are bursting with fresh flavors and are perfect for summer gatherings or picnics. Enjoy!

Spinach and Ricotta Stuffed Shells

Ingredients:

- 1 box (12 ounces) jumbo pasta shells
- 2 tablespoons olive oil
- 3 cloves garlic, minced
- 1 (10-ounce) package frozen chopped spinach, thawed and drained
- 1 container (15 ounces) ricotta cheese
- 1 cup shredded mozzarella cheese, divided
- 1/2 cup grated Parmesan cheese, plus extra for serving
- 1 large egg
- 1 teaspoon dried oregano
- 1 teaspoon dried basil
- Salt and pepper to taste
- 2 cups marinara sauce

Instructions:

1. Preheat your oven to 350°F (175°C). Grease a 9x13-inch baking dish with cooking spray or olive oil.
2. Cook the jumbo pasta shells according to the package instructions until they are al dente. Drain the shells and rinse them under cold water to stop the cooking process. Set aside.
3. In a large skillet, heat the olive oil over medium heat. Add the minced garlic and cook for 1-2 minutes until fragrant.
4. Add the thawed and drained spinach to the skillet and cook for an additional 2-3 minutes, stirring occasionally, until the excess moisture evaporates. Remove from heat and let cool slightly.
5. In a large mixing bowl, combine the cooked spinach, ricotta cheese, 1/2 cup shredded mozzarella cheese, grated Parmesan cheese, egg, dried oregano, dried basil, salt, and pepper. Mix until well combined.
6. Spread half of the marinara sauce in the bottom of the prepared baking dish.
7. Stuff each cooked pasta shell with a generous spoonful of the spinach and ricotta mixture and place them in the baking dish on top of the marinara sauce.
8. Once all the shells are stuffed and arranged in the baking dish, spoon the remaining marinara sauce over the top of the shells.
9. Sprinkle the remaining 1/2 cup shredded mozzarella cheese over the top of the stuffed shells.

10. Cover the baking dish with aluminum foil and bake in the preheated oven for 25-30 minutes, or until the cheese is melted and bubbly.
11. Remove the foil and continue to bake for an additional 5-10 minutes, or until the cheese is golden brown and the edges are slightly crispy.
12. Once done, remove the stuffed shells from the oven and let them cool for a few minutes before serving.
13. Serve the spinach and ricotta stuffed shells hot, garnished with extra grated Parmesan cheese if desired.

These spinach and ricotta stuffed shells are creamy, cheesy, and packed with flavor, making them a family favorite that's sure to please everyone at the table. Enjoy!

Baked Eggplant Parmesan Bites

Ingredients:

- 1 large eggplant, sliced into 1/4-inch thick rounds
- 1 cup all-purpose flour
- 2 large eggs, beaten
- 1 cup Italian-style breadcrumbs
- 1/2 cup grated Parmesan cheese
- 1 teaspoon dried oregano
- 1 teaspoon dried basil
- 1/2 teaspoon garlic powder
- Salt and pepper to taste
- Olive oil cooking spray
- Marinara sauce, for dipping
- Fresh basil leaves, chopped (for garnish)

Instructions:

1. Preheat your oven to 400°F (200°C). Line a baking sheet with parchment paper or lightly grease it with olive oil.
2. Prepare three shallow bowls. Place the all-purpose flour in the first bowl, the beaten eggs in the second bowl, and the Italian-style breadcrumbs mixed with grated Parmesan cheese, dried oregano, dried basil, garlic powder, salt, and pepper in the third bowl.
3. Dip each eggplant round into the flour, shaking off any excess. Then dip it into the beaten eggs, allowing any excess to drip off. Finally, coat it in the breadcrumb mixture, pressing gently to adhere.
4. Place the breaded eggplant rounds on the prepared baking sheet in a single layer.
5. Lightly spray the tops of the breaded eggplant rounds with olive oil cooking spray.
6. Bake the eggplant rounds in the preheated oven for 20-25 minutes, flipping halfway through, or until they are golden brown and crispy.
7. Once done, remove the baked eggplant rounds from the oven and let them cool slightly.
8. Serve the baked eggplant Parmesan bites hot, with marinara sauce for dipping.
9. Garnish with chopped fresh basil leaves for added flavor and presentation.

These baked eggplant Parmesan bites are crispy on the outside, tender on the inside, and bursting with Italian flavors. They make a fantastic appetizer or snack for any occasion. Enjoy!

Italian Sausage and Pepper Skewers

Ingredients:

- 1 pound Italian sausage (sweet or hot), cut into chunks
- 1 large red bell pepper, cut into chunks
- 1 large green bell pepper, cut into chunks
- 1 large yellow onion, cut into chunks
- 1 tablespoon olive oil
- 1 teaspoon Italian seasoning
- Salt and pepper to taste
- Wooden or metal skewers

Instructions:

1. If you're using wooden skewers, soak them in water for at least 30 minutes to prevent them from burning during cooking.
2. Preheat your grill to medium-high heat or preheat your oven to 400°F (200°C).
3. In a large bowl, toss the Italian sausage chunks, bell pepper chunks, and onion chunks with olive oil, Italian seasoning, salt, and pepper until evenly coated.
4. Thread the sausage, bell pepper, and onion chunks onto the skewers, alternating the ingredients as desired.
5. If grilling: Place the skewers on the preheated grill and cook for about 12-15 minutes, turning occasionally, or until the sausage is cooked through and the vegetables are tender and slightly charred. If baking: Place the skewers on a baking sheet lined with parchment paper or aluminum foil. Bake in the preheated oven for about 20-25 minutes, or until the sausage is cooked through and the vegetables are tender and slightly caramelized.
6. Once done, remove the skewers from the grill or oven and let them cool slightly.
7. Serve the Italian sausage and pepper skewers hot, either as a main dish with a side of pasta or as an appetizer with marinara sauce for dipping.

These Italian sausage and pepper skewers are flavorful, colorful, and easy to make, making them perfect for weeknight dinners or summer BBQs. Enjoy!

Garlic Shrimp Bruschetta

Ingredients:

- 1 French baguette, sliced into 1/2-inch thick rounds
- 1 pound large shrimp, peeled and deveined
- 3 cloves garlic, minced
- 2 tablespoons olive oil, divided
- Salt and pepper to taste
- 1 tablespoon fresh lemon juice
- 1 tablespoon chopped fresh parsley
- 1 cup cherry tomatoes, halved
- 1/4 cup grated Parmesan cheese (optional)
- Balsamic glaze (optional), for drizzling
- Fresh basil leaves, for garnish

Instructions:

1. Preheat your oven to 375°F (190°C). Place the baguette slices on a baking sheet in a single layer.
2. In a small bowl, mix together 1 tablespoon of olive oil and minced garlic. Brush the garlic oil mixture over the baguette slices.
3. Bake the baguette slices in the preheated oven for about 8-10 minutes, or until they are lightly toasted and golden brown. Keep an eye on them to prevent burning. Once done, remove them from the oven and set aside.
4. In a large skillet, heat the remaining tablespoon of olive oil over medium heat. Add the shrimp to the skillet and season with salt and pepper to taste. Cook the shrimp for 2-3 minutes on each side, or until they are pink and opaque.
5. Once the shrimp are cooked, remove them from the skillet and transfer them to a cutting board. Chop the shrimp into bite-sized pieces and place them in a mixing bowl.
6. To the bowl with the chopped shrimp, add the fresh lemon juice, chopped parsley, and halved cherry tomatoes. Toss everything together until well combined.
7. Spoon the shrimp mixture onto the toasted baguette slices, dividing it evenly among them.
8. If desired, sprinkle grated Parmesan cheese over the top of each shrimp bruschetta.
9. Drizzle balsamic glaze over the shrimp bruschetta for added flavor and presentation, if desired.
10. Garnish each shrimp bruschetta with fresh basil leaves.
11. Serve the garlic shrimp bruschetta immediately as a delicious appetizer or light meal.

These garlic shrimp bruschetta are bursting with flavor and make for an impressive and satisfying dish that's perfect for entertaining or enjoying as a snack. Enjoy!

Tomato and Mozzarella Tartlets

Ingredients:

For the tartlet shells:

- 1 sheet puff pastry, thawed
- Flour, for dusting

For the filling:

- 2-3 medium tomatoes, sliced
- 1-2 balls fresh mozzarella cheese, sliced
- Fresh basil leaves
- Salt and pepper to taste
- Olive oil for drizzling

Instructions:

1. Preheat your oven to 400°F (200°C). Line a baking sheet with parchment paper.
2. On a lightly floured surface, roll out the puff pastry sheet to about 1/4 inch thickness. Use a round cookie cutter or a glass to cut out circles from the puff pastry.
3. Place the puff pastry circles on the prepared baking sheet. Using a fork, prick the centers of the pastry circles to prevent them from puffing up too much during baking.
4. Bake the tartlet shells in the preheated oven for 12-15 minutes, or until they are golden brown and crispy. Remove them from the oven and let them cool slightly.
5. While the tartlet shells are baking, prepare the filling. Slice the tomatoes and fresh mozzarella cheese into thin slices.
6. Once the tartlet shells have cooled slightly, top each one with a slice of tomato, a slice of mozzarella cheese, and a fresh basil leaf. Season with salt and pepper to taste.
7. Drizzle a little olive oil over the top of each tartlet.
8. Return the assembled tartlets to the oven and bake for an additional 5-7 minutes, or until the cheese is melted and bubbly.
9. Once done, remove the tomato and mozzarella tartlets from the oven and let them cool slightly before serving.
10. Serve the tartlets warm as a delicious appetizer or snack.

These tomato and mozzarella tartlets are simple to make yet elegant and bursting with fresh flavors. Enjoy!

Mini Meatball Sliders

Ingredients:

For the meatballs:

- 1 pound ground beef (or a mixture of beef and pork)
- 1/2 cup breadcrumbs
- 1/4 cup grated Parmesan cheese
- 1 egg
- 2 cloves garlic, minced
- 1 teaspoon dried oregano
- 1 teaspoon dried basil
- Salt and pepper to taste
- Olive oil, for frying

For assembly:

- Mini slider buns
- Marinara sauce
- Mozzarella cheese slices (optional)
- Fresh basil leaves (optional)

Instructions:

1. Preheat your oven to 375°F (190°C).
2. In a large mixing bowl, combine the ground beef, breadcrumbs, grated Parmesan cheese, egg, minced garlic, dried oregano, dried basil, salt, and pepper. Mix until well combined.
3. Shape the meat mixture into small meatballs, about 1 inch in diameter.
4. Heat a drizzle of olive oil in a large skillet over medium heat. Add the meatballs in batches and cook for 2-3 minutes per side, or until browned on all sides. Transfer the browned meatballs to a baking sheet lined with parchment paper.
5. Once all the meatballs are browned, transfer the baking sheet to the preheated oven and bake for an additional 10-12 minutes, or until the meatballs are cooked through.
6. While the meatballs are baking, prepare the slider buns by slicing them in half horizontally. Optionally, you can lightly toast the buns in the oven for a few minutes.
7. Once the meatballs are done baking, remove them from the oven and assemble the sliders. Place a meatball on the bottom half of each slider bun. Top each meatball with a spoonful of marinara sauce and a slice of mozzarella cheese, if desired.
8. Place the top half of the slider buns on top of the meatballs.
9. Optionally, garnish each slider with a fresh basil leaf.

10. Serve the mini meatball sliders warm, and enjoy!

These mini meatball sliders are sure to be a hit at your next party or gathering. They're flavorful, satisfying, and perfect for sharing with friends and family.

Ricotta and Spinach Stuffed Mushrooms

Ingredients:

- 20-24 large mushrooms, cleaned with stems removed
- 1 cup ricotta cheese
- 1 cup chopped spinach, cooked and drained
- 1/2 cup grated Parmesan cheese
- 2 cloves garlic, minced
- 1/2 teaspoon dried oregano
- 1/2 teaspoon dried basil
- Salt and pepper to taste
- Olive oil for drizzling
- Fresh parsley, chopped (for garnish)

Instructions:

1. Preheat your oven to 375°F (190°C). Line a baking sheet with parchment paper or lightly grease it with olive oil.
2. In a mixing bowl, combine the ricotta cheese, chopped spinach, grated Parmesan cheese, minced garlic, dried oregano, dried basil, salt, and pepper. Mix until well combined.
3. Spoon the ricotta and spinach mixture into the cleaned mushroom caps, filling each one generously.
4. Place the stuffed mushrooms on the prepared baking sheet.
5. Drizzle a little olive oil over the stuffed mushrooms.
6. Bake the stuffed mushrooms in the preheated oven for 20-25 minutes, or until the mushrooms are tender and the filling is golden brown and bubbly.
7. Once done, remove the stuffed mushrooms from the oven and let them cool slightly.
8. Garnish the stuffed mushrooms with chopped fresh parsley for added flavor and presentation.
9. Serve the ricotta and spinach stuffed mushrooms warm as a delicious appetizer.

These ricotta and spinach stuffed mushrooms are creamy, flavorful, and sure to impress your guests. Enjoy!

Crostini with Goat Cheese and Roasted Red Peppers

Ingredients:

- Baguette, sliced into 1/2-inch thick rounds
- Olive oil, for drizzling
- 4 ounces soft goat cheese
- 1 large roasted red pepper, sliced into strips
- Fresh basil leaves, for garnish
- Balsamic glaze, for drizzling (optional)
- Salt and pepper to taste

Instructions:

1. Preheat your oven to 375°F (190°C). Place the baguette slices on a baking sheet in a single layer.
2. Drizzle olive oil over the baguette slices and sprinkle with salt and pepper.
3. Bake the baguette slices in the preheated oven for about 8-10 minutes, or until they are lightly toasted and golden brown. Keep an eye on them to prevent burning. Once done, remove them from the oven and let them cool slightly.
4. Once the baguette slices have cooled slightly, spread a generous layer of soft goat cheese onto each slice.
5. Top each crostini with a strip of roasted red pepper.
6. Garnish each crostini with a fresh basil leaf.
7. Optionally, drizzle balsamic glaze over the top of each crostini for added flavor and presentation.
8. Serve the crostini with goat cheese and roasted red peppers immediately as a delicious appetizer.

These crostini are perfect for entertaining and are sure to impress your guests with their vibrant colors and delicious flavors. Enjoy!

Polenta Crostini with Gorgonzola and Honey

Ingredients:

- 1 tube of prepared polenta, sliced into 1/2-inch thick rounds
- Olive oil, for drizzling
- 4 ounces gorgonzola cheese, crumbled
- Honey, for drizzling
- Fresh thyme leaves, for garnish (optional)

Instructions:

1. Preheat your oven to 375°F (190°C). Line a baking sheet with parchment paper.
2. Place the sliced polenta rounds on the prepared baking sheet in a single layer.
3. Drizzle olive oil over the polenta rounds.
4. Bake the polenta rounds in the preheated oven for about 15-20 minutes, or until they are lightly golden and crispy around the edges.
5. Once the polenta rounds are done baking, remove them from the oven and let them cool slightly.
6. Top each polenta round with crumbled gorgonzola cheese.
7. Drizzle honey over the top of each polenta round, to taste.
8. Optionally, garnish each polenta crostini with fresh thyme leaves for added flavor and presentation.
9. Serve the polenta crostini with gorgonzola and honey immediately as a delicious appetizer.

These polenta crostini are rich, creamy, and bursting with flavor, making them a perfect addition to any party or gathering. Enjoy!

Zucchini Fritters with Garlic Aioli

Ingredients:

For the zucchini fritters:

- 2 medium zucchinis, grated
- 1 teaspoon salt
- 2 large eggs
- 1/4 cup all-purpose flour
- 1/4 cup grated Parmesan cheese
- 2 cloves garlic, minced
- 1 tablespoon chopped fresh parsley (optional)
- Salt and pepper to taste
- Olive oil for frying

For the garlic aioli:

- 1/2 cup mayonnaise
- 1 clove garlic, minced
- 1 tablespoon lemon juice
- Salt and pepper to taste

Instructions:

1. Start by grating the zucchinis using a box grater or a food processor. Place the grated zucchini in a colander set over a bowl and sprinkle with 1 teaspoon of salt. Let it sit for about 10-15 minutes to allow excess moisture to drain from the zucchini.
2. After the zucchini has released some moisture, use your hands to squeeze out any remaining liquid. Transfer the squeezed zucchini to a clean kitchen towel and squeeze out any additional moisture.
3. In a large mixing bowl, combine the grated zucchini, eggs, all-purpose flour, grated Parmesan cheese, minced garlic, chopped fresh parsley (if using), salt, and pepper. Mix until well combined.
4. Heat a thin layer of olive oil in a large skillet over medium heat.
5. Once the oil is hot, scoop about 2 tablespoons of the zucchini mixture and form it into a patty. Place the patty in the skillet and flatten it slightly with a spatula. Repeat with the remaining zucchini mixture, making sure not to overcrowd the skillet.
6. Fry the zucchini fritters for 2-3 minutes on each side, or until they are golden brown and crispy. You may need to work in batches depending on the size of your skillet.
7. Once the zucchini fritters are cooked, transfer them to a plate lined with paper towels to drain any excess oil.

8. To make the garlic aioli, whisk together the mayonnaise, minced garlic, lemon juice, salt, and pepper in a small bowl until smooth and well combined.
9. Serve the zucchini fritters warm with the garlic aioli on the side for dipping.

These zucchini fritters with garlic aioli are crispy on the outside, tender on the inside, and packed with flavor. Enjoy!

Caprese Stuffed Avocado

Ingredients:

- 2 ripe avocados
- 1 cup cherry tomatoes, halved
- 4 ounces fresh mozzarella cheese, diced
- Fresh basil leaves, chopped
- Balsamic glaze, for drizzling
- Extra virgin olive oil, for drizzling
- Salt and pepper to taste

Instructions:

1. Cut the avocados in half lengthwise and remove the pits. Scoop out a little bit of the flesh from each avocado half to create a larger cavity for the filling.
2. In a mixing bowl, combine the halved cherry tomatoes, diced fresh mozzarella cheese, and chopped fresh basil leaves. Season with salt and pepper to taste.
3. Spoon the tomato and mozzarella mixture into the hollowed-out cavities of the avocado halves, dividing it evenly among them.
4. Drizzle a little balsamic glaze and extra virgin olive oil over the stuffed avocados.
5. Optionally, garnish the stuffed avocados with additional chopped basil leaves for added flavor and presentation.
6. Serve the Caprese stuffed avocados immediately as a delicious appetizer or light meal.

These Caprese stuffed avocados are fresh, flavorful, and perfect for summer entertaining.

Enjoy!

Italian Wedding Soup Shooters

Ingredients:

For the meatballs:

- 1/2 pound ground beef
- 1/4 cup breadcrumbs
- 1/4 cup grated Parmesan cheese
- 1 egg
- 1 clove garlic, minced
- 1 tablespoon chopped fresh parsley
- Salt and pepper to taste

For the soup:

- 6 cups chicken broth
- 1 cup small pasta (such as acini di pepe or orzo)
- 2 cups baby spinach leaves
- Salt and pepper to taste

Instructions:

1. To make the meatballs, in a mixing bowl, combine the ground beef, breadcrumbs, grated Parmesan cheese, egg, minced garlic, chopped fresh parsley, salt, and pepper. Mix until well combined.
2. Roll the mixture into small meatballs, about 1-inch in diameter.
3. In a large pot, bring the chicken broth to a simmer over medium heat. Add the small pasta to the pot and cook according to the package instructions until al dente.
4. Once the pasta is cooked, add the meatballs to the pot and simmer for about 10-12 minutes, or until the meatballs are cooked through.
5. Stir in the baby spinach leaves and cook for an additional 1-2 minutes, or until wilted. Season the soup with salt and pepper to taste.
6. Ladle the soup into shot glasses or small cups, filling each one about halfway.
7. Optionally, garnish each soup shooter with a sprinkle of grated Parmesan cheese and chopped fresh parsley.
8. Serve the Italian wedding soup shooters immediately as a delicious appetizer.

These Italian wedding soup shooters are flavorful, comforting, and perfect for serving at any festive occasion. Enjoy!

Mini Margherita Pizzas

Ingredients:

- Mini pizza dough rounds or mini pizza bases
- Olive oil
- Tomato sauce or marinara sauce
- Fresh mozzarella cheese, sliced
- Fresh basil leaves
- Cherry tomatoes, halved
- Salt and pepper to taste

Instructions:

1. Preheat your oven to the temperature specified on the pizza dough package.
2. Place the mini pizza dough rounds or bases on a baking sheet lined with parchment paper.
3. Brush each pizza base lightly with olive oil.
4. Spread a thin layer of tomato sauce or marinara sauce over each pizza base.
5. Place a slice of fresh mozzarella cheese on top of the sauce on each pizza.
6. Arrange halved cherry tomatoes on top of the cheese.
7. Season the pizzas with a sprinkle of salt and pepper to taste.
8. Bake the mini Margherita pizzas in the preheated oven according to the instructions on the pizza dough package, or until the cheese is melted and bubbly and the crust is golden brown.
9. Once done, remove the pizzas from the oven and let them cool slightly.
10. Garnish each mini Margherita pizza with fresh basil leaves before serving.

These mini Margherita pizzas are flavorful, cheesy, and perfect for serving as an appetizer or party snack. Enjoy!

Grilled Artichoke Hearts with Lemon Garlic Aioli

Ingredients:

For the grilled artichoke hearts:

- 2 large artichokes
- 2 tablespoons olive oil
- Salt and pepper to taste
- Lemon wedges, for serving

For the lemon garlic aioli:

- 1/2 cup mayonnaise
- 1 clove garlic, minced
- 1 tablespoon fresh lemon juice
- 1 teaspoon lemon zest
- Salt and pepper to taste

Instructions:

1. Prepare the artichokes by trimming the stems and removing the tough outer leaves. Cut off the top third of each artichoke and use kitchen scissors to trim the sharp tips from the remaining leaves.
2. Bring a large pot of salted water to a boil. Add the artichokes and cook for about 20-30 minutes, or until the outer leaves can be easily pulled off and the base is tender when pierced with a knife. Drain the artichokes and let them cool slightly.
3. Once the artichokes are cool enough to handle, cut them in half lengthwise and use a spoon to scoop out the fuzzy choke from the center.
4. Preheat your grill to medium-high heat.
5. Brush the cut sides of the artichoke halves with olive oil and season with salt and pepper.
6. Place the artichokes cut side down on the preheated grill and cook for about 5-7 minutes, or until lightly charred and heated through. Flip the artichokes and grill for an additional 2-3 minutes.
7. While the artichokes are grilling, prepare the lemon garlic aioli. In a small bowl, whisk together the mayonnaise, minced garlic, fresh lemon juice, lemon zest, salt, and pepper until smooth and well combined.
8. Once the artichokes are grilled to your liking, remove them from the grill and transfer them to a serving platter.
9. Serve the grilled artichoke hearts hot, with lemon wedges and the lemon garlic aioli on the side for dipping.

These grilled artichoke hearts with lemon garlic aioli are flavorful, tender, and perfect for summer entertaining. Enjoy!

Olive Tapenade Crostini

Ingredients:

For the olive tapenade:

- 1 cup pitted black olives
- 1/4 cup pitted Kalamata olives
- 2 cloves garlic, minced
- 2 tablespoons capers, drained
- 2 tablespoons chopped fresh parsley
- 1 tablespoon lemon juice
- 2 tablespoons extra virgin olive oil
- Salt and pepper to taste

For the crostini:

- Baguette, sliced into 1/2-inch thick rounds
- Olive oil
- Salt and pepper to taste

Instructions:

1. Preheat your oven to 375°F (190°C). Line a baking sheet with parchment paper.
2. To make the olive tapenade, combine the black olives, Kalamata olives, minced garlic, capers, chopped fresh parsley, lemon juice, and extra virgin olive oil in a food processor. Pulse until the mixture reaches your desired consistency. You can leave it slightly chunky or blend it until smooth. Season with salt and pepper to taste.
3. Place the baguette slices on the prepared baking sheet in a single layer.
4. Brush each baguette slice lightly with olive oil and season with salt and pepper.
5. Bake the crostini in the preheated oven for about 8-10 minutes, or until they are lightly golden and crispy. Keep an eye on them to prevent burning. Once done, remove them from the oven and let them cool slightly.
6. Once the crostini are cooled, spread a generous layer of olive tapenade onto each slice.
7. Serve the olive tapenade crostini immediately as a delicious appetizer.

These olive tapenade crostini are packed with flavor and make a perfect addition to any party or gathering. Enjoy!

Baked Zucchini Parmesan Chips

Ingredients:

- 2 medium zucchinis, thinly sliced into rounds
- 1/2 cup grated Parmesan cheese
- 1/2 cup breadcrumbs (you can use regular or Panko breadcrumbs)
- 1 teaspoon Italian seasoning (optional)
- 1/2 teaspoon garlic powder
- Salt and pepper to taste
- 2 large eggs, beaten
- Olive oil cooking spray

Instructions:

1. Preheat your oven to 425°F (220°C). Line a baking sheet with parchment paper or aluminum foil and lightly coat it with olive oil cooking spray.
2. In a shallow dish, combine the grated Parmesan cheese, breadcrumbs, Italian seasoning (if using), garlic powder, salt, and pepper. Mix well to combine.
3. Dip each zucchini slice into the beaten eggs, then dredge it in the breadcrumb mixture, pressing gently to coat both sides evenly. Shake off any excess breadcrumbs.
4. Place the coated zucchini slices in a single layer on the prepared baking sheet.
5. Lightly spray the tops of the zucchini slices with olive oil cooking spray to help them crisp up in the oven.
6. Bake the zucchini Parmesan chips in the preheated oven for 20-25 minutes, flipping them halfway through, or until they are golden brown and crispy.
7. Once done, remove the zucchini chips from the oven and let them cool slightly before serving.
8. Serve the baked zucchini Parmesan chips warm as a delicious and healthy snack.

These baked zucchini Parmesan chips are crispy, flavorful, and addictive, making them a perfect guilt-free snack or appetizer. Enjoy!

Ricotta and Tomato Bruschetta

Ingredients:

- 1 baguette, sliced into 1/2-inch thick rounds
- Olive oil
- 1 cup cherry tomatoes, halved
- 1/2 cup ricotta cheese
- 1 clove garlic, minced
- 1 tablespoon fresh basil, chopped
- Salt and pepper to taste
- Balsamic glaze for drizzling (optional)

Instructions:

1. Preheat your oven to 375°F (190°C). Arrange the baguette slices on a baking sheet lined with parchment paper.
2. Lightly brush each baguette slice with olive oil on both sides.
3. Bake the baguette slices in the preheated oven for about 8-10 minutes, or until they are lightly toasted and golden brown. Keep an eye on them to prevent burning. Once done, remove them from the oven and let them cool slightly.
4. In a small mixing bowl, combine the ricotta cheese, minced garlic, chopped basil, salt, and pepper. Mix until well combined.
5. Spread a generous layer of the ricotta mixture onto each toasted baguette slice.
6. Top each bruschetta with halved cherry tomatoes.
7. Optionally, drizzle balsamic glaze over the top of each bruschetta for added flavor and presentation.
8. Serve the ricotta and tomato bruschetta immediately as a delicious appetizer.

This ricotta and tomato bruschetta is fresh, creamy, and bursting with flavor, making it a perfect starter for any meal or party. Enjoy!

Grilled Prosciutto-Wrapped Figs

Ingredients:

- 8 fresh figs, ripe but firm
- 8 slices prosciutto
- Balsamic glaze (optional), for drizzling
- Fresh basil leaves (optional), for garnish

Instructions:

1. Preheat your grill to medium-high heat.
2. While the grill is heating up, prepare the figs by cutting a small slit in the top of each fig, making sure not to cut all the way through. This will create a pocket for the prosciutto.
3. Wrap each fig with a slice of prosciutto, securing it around the fig. You can tear the prosciutto into smaller strips if needed to cover the figs completely.
4. Place the prosciutto-wrapped figs on the preheated grill, cut-side down.
5. Grill the figs for about 2-3 minutes per side, or until the prosciutto is crispy and the figs are slightly softened and caramelized.
6. Once done, remove the grilled prosciutto-wrapped figs from the grill and transfer them to a serving platter.
7. Optionally, drizzle balsamic glaze over the top of the grilled figs for added flavor and presentation.
8. Garnish the grilled figs with fresh basil leaves for a pop of color and extra freshness.
9. Serve the grilled prosciutto-wrapped figs immediately as a delicious appetizer or snack.

These grilled prosciutto-wrapped figs are a perfect combination of sweet and savory flavors, making them a hit at any gathering or party. Enjoy!

Parmesan and Herb Puff Pastry Twists

Ingredients:

- 1 sheet puff pastry, thawed
- 1/4 cup grated Parmesan cheese
- 2 tablespoons finely chopped fresh herbs (such as parsley, thyme, or rosemary)
- 1/2 teaspoon garlic powder
- Salt and pepper to taste
- 1 egg, beaten (for egg wash)

Instructions:

1. Preheat your oven to 400°F (200°C). Line a baking sheet with parchment paper.
2. In a small bowl, mix together the grated Parmesan cheese, chopped fresh herbs, garlic powder, salt, and pepper. Set aside.
3. Unroll the thawed puff pastry sheet onto a lightly floured surface.
4. Brush the surface of the puff pastry sheet with the beaten egg.
5. Sprinkle the Parmesan and herb mixture evenly over the egg-washed puff pastry sheet.
6. Gently press the Parmesan and herb mixture into the puff pastry to adhere.
7. Using a sharp knife or pizza cutter, cut the puff pastry sheet into thin strips, about 1/2 inch wide.
8. Twist each strip of puff pastry several times to create a spiral shape, then place it onto the prepared baking sheet, pressing down the ends lightly to prevent unraveling.
9. Repeat with the remaining strips of puff pastry.
10. Bake the Parmesan and herb puff pastry twists in the preheated oven for 12-15 minutes, or until they are golden brown and crispy.
11. Once done, remove the puff pastry twists from the oven and let them cool slightly before serving.
12. Serve the Parmesan and herb puff pastry twists warm as a delicious appetizer or snack.

These puff pastry twists are buttery, cheesy, and packed with aromatic herbs, making them irresistible for any occasion. Enjoy!

Fried Ravioli with Marinara Sauce

Ingredients:

- 1 package store-bought cheese ravioli (fresh or frozen)
- 2 eggs, beaten
- 1 cup Italian breadcrumbs
- 1/2 cup grated Parmesan cheese
- 1 teaspoon Italian seasoning
- 1/2 teaspoon garlic powder
- Salt and pepper to taste
- Olive oil for frying
- Marinara sauce for dipping

Instructions:

1. Cook the ravioli according to the package instructions until they are just tender. Drain them well and let them cool slightly.
2. In a shallow dish, combine the Italian breadcrumbs, grated Parmesan cheese, Italian seasoning, garlic powder, salt, and pepper. Mix well to combine.
3. Dip each cooked ravioli into the beaten eggs, then coat it in the breadcrumb mixture, pressing gently to adhere the breadcrumbs to the ravioli. Repeat with the remaining ravioli.
4. Heat a generous amount of olive oil in a large skillet over medium heat.
5. Once the oil is hot, carefully add the breaded ravioli to the skillet in batches, making sure not to overcrowd the pan. Fry the ravioli for 2-3 minutes per side, or until they are golden brown and crispy.
6. Once done, use a slotted spoon to transfer the fried ravioli to a plate lined with paper towels to drain any excess oil.
7. Serve the fried ravioli immediately with marinara sauce for dipping.

These fried ravioli with marinara sauce are crispy on the outside, creamy and cheesy on the inside, and perfect for snacking or entertaining. Enjoy!

Italian Stuffed Bell Peppers

Ingredients:

- 4 large bell peppers (any color), halved and seeds removed
- 1 tablespoon olive oil
- 1 onion, diced
- 2 cloves garlic, minced
- 1 pound ground Italian sausage (or ground beef or turkey)
- 1 cup cooked rice (white or brown)
- 1 cup marinara sauce
- 1 teaspoon Italian seasoning
- Salt and pepper to taste
- 1 cup shredded mozzarella cheese
- Fresh basil leaves, chopped (for garnish)

Instructions:

1. Preheat your oven to 375°F (190°C). Place the halved bell peppers in a baking dish, cut side up.
2. In a large skillet, heat the olive oil over medium heat. Add the diced onion and minced garlic, and sauté until softened, about 2-3 minutes.
3. Add the ground Italian sausage to the skillet and cook until browned, breaking it up into smaller pieces with a spatula.
4. Stir in the cooked rice, marinara sauce, Italian seasoning, salt, and pepper. Cook for an additional 2-3 minutes, allowing the flavors to meld together.
5. Spoon the sausage and rice mixture evenly into the halved bell peppers, pressing down gently to pack the filling.
6. Cover the baking dish with aluminum foil and bake in the preheated oven for 25-30 minutes, or until the bell peppers are tender.
7. Remove the foil from the baking dish and sprinkle the shredded mozzarella cheese evenly over the top of each stuffed bell pepper.
8. Return the baking dish to the oven and bake for an additional 5-7 minutes, or until the cheese is melted and bubbly.
9. Once done, remove the stuffed bell peppers from the oven and let them cool slightly before serving.
10. Garnish the stuffed bell peppers with chopped fresh basil leaves before serving.

These Italian stuffed bell peppers are hearty, flavorful, and perfect for a comforting weeknight meal. Enjoy!

Roasted Red Pepper and Feta Bruschetta

Ingredients:

- 1 baguette, sliced into 1/2-inch thick rounds
- Olive oil
- 2 roasted red peppers, sliced into strips
- 4 ounces feta cheese, crumbled
- 2 tablespoons fresh parsley, chopped
- 1 tablespoon balsamic vinegar
- Salt and pepper to taste

Instructions:

1. Preheat your oven to 375°F (190°C). Place the baguette slices on a baking sheet in a single layer.
2. Brush each baguette slice lightly with olive oil on both sides.
3. Bake the baguette slices in the preheated oven for about 8-10 minutes, or until they are lightly toasted and golden brown. Keep an eye on them to prevent burning. Once done, remove them from the oven and let them cool slightly.
4. In a small mixing bowl, combine the roasted red pepper strips, crumbled feta cheese, chopped fresh parsley, balsamic vinegar, salt, and pepper. Mix until well combined.
5. Spoon the roasted red pepper and feta mixture onto each toasted baguette slice, dividing it evenly among them.
6. Serve the roasted red pepper and feta bruschetta immediately as a delicious appetizer.

These bruschetta are bursting with flavor, with the sweetness of the roasted red peppers complementing the tanginess of the feta cheese. They're perfect for serving at parties or gatherings. Enjoy!

Caprese Skewers with Balsamic Glaze

Ingredients:

- Cherry or grape tomatoes
- Fresh mozzarella cheese, cut into bite-sized cubes
- Fresh basil leaves
- Balsamic glaze
- Wooden skewers

Instructions:

1. Assemble the skewers by threading a cherry tomato, a cube of fresh mozzarella cheese, and a fresh basil leaf onto each wooden skewer. Repeat until all ingredients are used, alternating between the tomatoes, cheese, and basil leaves.
2. Arrange the assembled skewers on a serving platter.
3. Drizzle balsamic glaze over the top of the skewers, creating a decorative pattern.
4. Serve the Caprese skewers with balsamic glaze immediately as a delicious appetizer.

These Caprese skewers with balsamic glaze are fresh, flavorful, and visually appealing, making them a perfect addition to any party or gathering. Enjoy!

Mushroom and Fontina Arancini

Ingredients:

For the arancini:

- 2 cups Arborio rice
- 4 cups chicken or vegetable broth
- 1 tablespoon olive oil
- 1 onion, finely chopped
- 2 cloves garlic, minced
- 8 ounces mushrooms (such as cremini or button), finely chopped
- 1/2 cup dry white wine (optional)
- 1 cup grated Fontina cheese
- Salt and pepper to taste
- 2 eggs, beaten
- 1 cup breadcrumbs
- Vegetable oil, for frying

For serving (optional):

- Marinara sauce
- Fresh basil leaves

Instructions:

1. In a large saucepan, heat the chicken or vegetable broth over medium heat until simmering.
2. In another large saucepan or Dutch oven, heat the olive oil over medium heat. Add the chopped onion and garlic, and sauté until softened and fragrant, about 2-3 minutes.
3. Add the Arborio rice to the saucepan with the onions and garlic. Cook, stirring constantly, for 1-2 minutes until the rice is well-coated with the oil and slightly translucent.
4. Gradually add the hot broth to the rice, one ladleful at a time, stirring constantly and allowing the liquid to absorb before adding more. Continue this process until the rice is creamy and cooked al dente, about 18-20 minutes. You may not need to use all of the broth.

5. In a separate skillet, heat a little olive oil over medium heat. Add the chopped mushrooms and sauté until they are tender and any liquid they release has evaporated, about 5-7 minutes. Season with salt and pepper to taste.
6. Once the rice is cooked, remove it from the heat and stir in the sautéed mushrooms and grated Fontina cheese until well combined. Taste and adjust seasoning if necessary.
7. Let the rice mixture cool slightly, then shape it into golf ball-sized balls, pressing a cube of Fontina cheese into the center of each ball as you form them.
8. Dip each arancini ball into the beaten eggs, then roll it in the breadcrumbs until coated evenly.
9. In a large skillet or deep fryer, heat vegetable oil to 350°F (180°C). Fry the arancini in batches until golden brown and crispy, about 3-4 minutes per batch. Use a slotted spoon to transfer the fried arancini to a plate lined with paper towels to drain any excess oil.
10. Serve the mushroom and Fontina arancini hot, optionally with marinara sauce for dipping and garnish with fresh basil leaves.

These mushroom and Fontina arancini are crispy on the outside, creamy and cheesy on the inside, and packed with delicious mushroom flavor. Enjoy this delightful Italian treat!

Caponata Crostini

Ingredients:

For the caponata:

- 1 large eggplant, diced into small cubes
- Salt
- Olive oil
- 1 onion, finely chopped
- 2 cloves garlic, minced
- 1 celery stalk, finely chopped
- 1 red bell pepper, diced
- 1 can (14 oz) diced tomatoes, drained
- 1/4 cup green olives, pitted and chopped
- 2 tablespoons capers, rinsed and drained
- 2 tablespoons red wine vinegar
- 2 tablespoons honey or sugar
- 1/4 cup fresh basil leaves, chopped
- Salt and pepper to taste

For the crostini:

- Baguette, sliced into 1/2-inch thick rounds
- Olive oil

Instructions:

1. Place the diced eggplant in a colander and sprinkle with salt. Let it sit for about 30 minutes to draw out excess moisture. Rinse the eggplant thoroughly and pat dry with paper towels.
2. Preheat your oven to 375°F (190°C). Arrange the baguette slices on a baking sheet and brush them lightly with olive oil. Bake in the preheated oven for about 8-10 minutes, or until they are golden and crispy. Remove from the oven and set aside.
3. In a large skillet, heat a few tablespoons of olive oil over medium heat. Add the diced eggplant and cook until softened and lightly browned, about 8-10 minutes. Remove the eggplant from the skillet and set aside.
4. In the same skillet, add a little more olive oil if needed and sauté the chopped onion, garlic, celery, and red bell pepper until softened, about 5-7 minutes.
5. Add the diced tomatoes, green olives, capers, red wine vinegar, and honey (or sugar) to the skillet. Stir to combine.

6. Return the cooked eggplant to the skillet and stir to combine with the other ingredients. Cook for an additional 5-7 minutes, allowing the flavors to meld together.
7. Stir in the chopped fresh basil leaves and season the caponata with salt and pepper to taste. Remove from heat and let it cool slightly.
8. To assemble the crostini, spoon a generous amount of caponata onto each toasted baguette slice.
9. Serve the caponata crostini at room temperature as a delicious appetizer or snack.

These caponata crostini are bursting with flavor, with the sweet and tangy eggplant relish complementing the crunchy bread perfectly. They're perfect for serving at parties or gatherings. Enjoy!

Sausage and Ricotta Stuffed Mushrooms

Ingredients:

- 24 large mushrooms, cleaned with stems removed
- 1 tablespoon olive oil
- 8 ounces Italian sausage, casings removed
- 1/2 onion, finely chopped
- 2 cloves garlic, minced
- 1/2 cup ricotta cheese
- 1/4 cup grated Parmesan cheese
- 2 tablespoons chopped fresh parsley
- Salt and pepper to taste
- 1/2 cup breadcrumbs
- 1/4 cup grated mozzarella cheese (optional, for topping)
- Fresh parsley leaves, for garnish

Instructions:

1. Preheat your oven to 375°F (190°C). Line a baking sheet with parchment paper.
2. In a large skillet, heat the olive oil over medium heat. Add the Italian sausage and cook, breaking it up with a spatula, until browned and cooked through, about 5-7 minutes.
3. Add the chopped onion and minced garlic to the skillet with the sausage and cook until the onion is softened, about 3-5 minutes. Remove from heat and let it cool slightly.
4. In a mixing bowl, combine the cooked sausage mixture with ricotta cheese, grated Parmesan cheese, chopped fresh parsley, salt, and pepper. Mix until well combined.
5. Spoon the sausage and ricotta mixture into each mushroom cap, filling them generously.
6. In a separate bowl, mix together the breadcrumbs with a little olive oil until the breadcrumbs are evenly coated.
7. Sprinkle the breadcrumbs over the stuffed mushrooms, pressing them lightly to adhere.
8. If desired, sprinkle grated mozzarella cheese over the top of each stuffed mushroom for extra cheesiness.

9. Arrange the stuffed mushrooms on the prepared baking sheet and bake in the preheated oven for 15-20 minutes, or until the mushrooms are tender and the filling is heated through and lightly browned on top.
10. Once done, remove the stuffed mushrooms from the oven and let them cool slightly before serving.
11. Garnish the stuffed mushrooms with fresh parsley leaves before serving.

These sausage and ricotta stuffed mushrooms are flavorful, cheesy, and irresistible. They make a perfect appetizer for any occasion. Enjoy!

Pesto Palmiers

Ingredients:

- 1 sheet puff pastry, thawed
- 1/2 cup basil pesto (homemade or store-bought)
- 1/4 cup grated Parmesan cheese
- Salt and pepper, to taste
- Olive oil (optional, for brushing)
- Flaky sea salt (optional, for garnish)

Instructions:

1. Preheat your oven to 400°F (200°C). Line a baking sheet with parchment paper.
2. On a lightly floured surface, roll out the thawed puff pastry sheet into a rectangle.
3. Spread the basil pesto evenly over the puff pastry sheet, leaving a small border around the edges.
4. Sprinkle the grated Parmesan cheese over the pesto layer. Season with salt and pepper to taste.
5. Starting from one of the long edges, tightly roll the puff pastry sheet into a log, stopping at the middle.
6. Repeat the rolling process starting from the other long edge, until you have two rolls meeting in the middle, resembling a palmier.
7. Using a sharp knife, slice the rolled puff pastry log into 1/2-inch thick slices.
8. Place the slices cut-side down on the prepared baking sheet, spacing them slightly apart.
9. If desired, lightly brush the tops of the palmiers with olive oil for extra crispiness.
10. Bake the pesto palmiers in the preheated oven for 12-15 minutes, or until they are golden brown and puffed up.
11. Optional: Sprinkle the baked palmiers with flaky sea salt for extra flavor and presentation.
12. Remove the pesto palmiers from the oven and let them cool slightly on the baking sheet before serving.

These pesto palmiers are crispy, flaky, and bursting with savory pesto flavor. They make a perfect appetizer or snack for any occasion. Enjoy!

Tomato Basil Bruschetta Cups

Ingredients:

- 1 French baguette
- Olive oil
- 2 cups cherry tomatoes, diced
- 2 cloves garlic, minced
- 1/4 cup fresh basil, chopped
- 1 tablespoon balsamic vinegar
- Salt and pepper, to taste
- Grated Parmesan cheese (optional, for garnish)
- Balsamic glaze (optional, for garnish)

Instructions:

1. Preheat your oven to 375°F (190°C). Lightly grease a mini muffin tin with olive oil or non-stick cooking spray.
2. Slice the French baguette into 1/2-inch thick rounds. Using a small round cutter or the rim of a shot glass, cut each round into smaller circles that will fit into the mini muffin tin cups.
3. Place each baguette circle into the cups of the mini muffin tin, pressing down gently to form cups. Brush the tops of the baguette cups with olive oil.
4. Bake the baguette cups in the preheated oven for about 8-10 minutes, or until they are golden brown and crispy. Remove from the oven and let them cool slightly.
5. In a mixing bowl, combine the diced cherry tomatoes, minced garlic, chopped fresh basil, balsamic vinegar, salt, and pepper. Mix until well combined.
6. Spoon the tomato basil mixture into each baguette cup, filling them generously.
7. If desired, sprinkle grated Parmesan cheese over the top of each bruschetta cup for added flavor.
8. Optional: Drizzle balsamic glaze over the top of each bruschetta cup for extra sweetness and presentation.
9. Serve the tomato basil bruschetta cups immediately as a delicious appetizer or snack.

These tomato basil bruschetta cups are fresh, flavorful, and perfect for entertaining. They're sure to be a hit at any party or gathering. Enjoy!

Italian Stuffed Artichokes

Ingredients:

- 4 large artichokes
- 1 lemon, halved
- 1/2 cup breadcrumbs
- 1/4 cup grated Parmesan cheese
- 2 cloves garlic, minced
- 2 tablespoons chopped fresh parsley
- 2 tablespoons chopped fresh basil
- 1/4 cup olive oil
- Salt and pepper to taste
- 1 cup vegetable or chicken broth

Instructions:

1. Preheat your oven to 375°F (190°C).
2. Prepare the artichokes by trimming off the stem and about 1 inch from the top of each artichoke. Use kitchen scissors to trim the sharp tips from the remaining leaves.
3. Use your fingers to gently spread apart the leaves of each artichoke to make room for the stuffing.
4. Rub the cut surfaces of the artichokes with a halved lemon to prevent browning.
5. In a mixing bowl, combine the breadcrumbs, grated Parmesan cheese, minced garlic, chopped fresh parsley, chopped fresh basil, olive oil, salt, and pepper. Mix well to combine.
6. Stuff the breadcrumb mixture between the leaves of each artichoke, pressing down gently to pack the stuffing.
7. Place the stuffed artichokes in a baking dish and pour the vegetable or chicken broth into the bottom of the dish.
8. Cover the baking dish with aluminum foil and bake in the preheated oven for about 1 hour, or until the artichokes are tender when pierced with a knife.
9. Once done, remove the foil from the baking dish and return the artichokes to the oven for an additional 10-15 minutes, or until the breadcrumb topping is golden brown and crispy.
10. Serve the Italian stuffed artichokes hot, garnished with additional chopped parsley or basil if desired.

These Italian stuffed artichokes are savory, flavorful, and a perfect addition to any Italian-inspired meal. Enjoy!

Sun-Dried Tomato and Olive Tapenade

Ingredients:

- 1 cup pitted black olives
- 1/2 cup sun-dried tomatoes (packed in oil), drained
- 2 cloves garlic, minced
- 2 tablespoons capers, drained
- 2 tablespoons fresh parsley, chopped
- 1 tablespoon fresh lemon juice
- 2 tablespoons extra virgin olive oil
- Salt and pepper to taste

Instructions:

1. In a food processor, combine the pitted black olives, sun-dried tomatoes, minced garlic, capers, chopped fresh parsley, and fresh lemon juice.
2. Pulse the ingredients until they are finely chopped and well combined, but not completely smooth. You want the tapenade to have some texture.
3. With the food processor running, gradually drizzle in the extra virgin olive oil until the tapenade reaches your desired consistency. You may need to add a little more olive oil if the tapenade is too thick.
4. Taste the tapenade and season with salt and pepper to taste. Keep in mind that the olives and capers are already salty, so you may not need much additional salt.
5. Transfer the sun-dried tomato and olive tapenade to a serving bowl.
6. Serve the tapenade immediately as a spread for bread or crackers, or as a topping for grilled meats, fish, or vegetables.
7. Store any leftover tapenade in an airtight container in the refrigerator for up to one week.

This sun-dried tomato and olive tapenade is rich, tangy, and packed with flavor. It's sure to be a hit at your next gathering! Enjoy!

Pesto and Sun-Dried Tomato Pinwheels

Ingredients:

- 1 sheet puff pastry, thawed
- 1/4 cup prepared pesto sauce
- 1/4 cup sun-dried tomatoes, chopped
- 1/4 cup grated Parmesan cheese
- 1/4 cup shredded mozzarella cheese
- Olive oil, for brushing (optional)
- Fresh basil leaves, for garnish (optional)

Instructions:

1. Preheat your oven to 375°F (190°C). Line a baking sheet with parchment paper.
2. On a lightly floured surface, roll out the thawed puff pastry sheet into a rectangle.
3. Spread the pesto sauce evenly over the puff pastry sheet, leaving a small border around the edges.
4. Sprinkle the chopped sun-dried tomatoes, grated Parmesan cheese, and shredded mozzarella cheese over the pesto layer.
5. Starting from one of the long edges, tightly roll the puff pastry sheet into a log.
6. Use a sharp knife to slice the rolled puff pastry log into 1/2-inch thick rounds.
7. Place the slices cut-side down on the prepared baking sheet, spacing them slightly apart.
8. Optional: Brush the tops of the pinwheels with olive oil for extra crispiness and flavor.
9. Bake the pinwheels in the preheated oven for 12-15 minutes, or until they are golden brown and puffed up.
10. Once done, remove the pinwheels from the oven and let them cool slightly on the baking sheet.
11. Garnish the pesto and sun-dried tomato pinwheels with fresh basil leaves before serving, if desired.

These pesto and sun-dried tomato pinwheels are crispy, cheesy, and bursting with flavor. They make a perfect appetizer for any occasion. Enjoy!

Ricotta and Spinach Stuffed Pasta Shells

Ingredients:

- 1 box (12 ounces) jumbo pasta shells
- 2 cups ricotta cheese
- 1 ½ cups shredded mozzarella cheese, divided
- 1 cup grated Parmesan cheese
- 1 large egg
- 1 cup chopped spinach (fresh or frozen, thawed and drained)
- 2 cloves garlic, minced
- 1 teaspoon dried oregano
- 1 teaspoon dried basil
- Salt and pepper, to taste
- 2 cups marinara sauce

Instructions:

1. Preheat your oven to 350°F (175°C).
2. Cook the jumbo pasta shells according to the package instructions until they are al dente. Drain and set aside.
3. In a large mixing bowl, combine the ricotta cheese, 1 cup of mozzarella cheese, Parmesan cheese, egg, chopped spinach, minced garlic, dried oregano, dried basil, salt, and pepper. Mix until well combined.
4. Spread a thin layer of marinara sauce on the bottom of a baking dish.
5. Using a spoon, stuff each cooked pasta shell with the ricotta-spinach mixture and place them in the baking dish.
6. Once all the shells are stuffed and arranged in the baking dish, spoon the remaining marinara sauce over the top of the shells.
7. Sprinkle the remaining ½ cup of mozzarella cheese over the sauce.
8. Cover the baking dish with foil and bake in the preheated oven for 25-30 minutes, or until the cheese is melted and bubbly.
9. Remove the foil and bake for an additional 5-10 minutes, or until the cheese is golden brown and the shells are heated through.
10. Remove from the oven and let it cool for a few minutes before serving.

Enjoy your ricotta and spinach stuffed pasta shells! They make for a comforting and satisfying meal, perfect for any occasion. Serve them with a side salad and garlic bread for a complete dinner.

Italian Cheese Fondue with Bread Cubes

Ingredients:

- 8 ounces Fontina cheese, grated
- 8 ounces Gruyère cheese, grated
- 1 tablespoon cornstarch
- 1 clove garlic, halved
- 1 cup dry white wine
- 1 tablespoon lemon juice
- 1 tablespoon brandy (optional)
- Pinch of nutmeg (optional)
- Salt and pepper to taste
- Cubed Italian bread, for dipping
- Assorted vegetables (such as cherry tomatoes, blanched broccoli florets, roasted bell peppers) for dipping

Instructions:

1. In a medium bowl, toss the grated Fontina and Gruyère cheeses with the cornstarch until evenly coated. This will help thicken the fondue.
2. Rub the inside of a fondue pot or a heavy-bottomed saucepan with the cut sides of the garlic clove. Then discard the garlic.
3. Place the pot or saucepan over medium heat. Pour in the white wine and lemon juice, and bring to a gentle simmer.
4. Gradually add the cheese mixture to the simmering liquid, stirring constantly in a figure-eight motion until the cheese is melted and smooth.
5. If using, stir in the brandy and nutmeg until well combined.
6. Season the fondue with salt and pepper to taste, adjusting as needed.
7. Reduce the heat to low to keep the fondue warm and smooth. If the fondue becomes too thick, you can add a splash of wine to thin it out.
8. Serve the Italian cheese fondue immediately alongside the cubed Italian bread and assorted vegetables for dipping.

Enjoy dipping the bread cubes and vegetables into the rich and creamy cheese fondue, savoring the flavors and warmth of this delightful dish!

Mini Calzones with Marinara Dipping Sauce

Ingredients:

For the Calzones:

- 1 pound pizza dough, homemade or store-bought
- 1 cup ricotta cheese
- 1 cup shredded mozzarella cheese
- ½ cup grated Parmesan cheese
- 1 cup chopped cooked spinach (fresh or frozen, thawed and drained)
- ½ teaspoon garlic powder
- ½ teaspoon dried oregano
- Salt and pepper to taste
- Olive oil, for brushing

For the Marinara Dipping Sauce:

- 1 tablespoon olive oil
- 2 cloves garlic, minced
- 1 can (14 ounces) crushed tomatoes
- 1 teaspoon dried basil
- 1 teaspoon dried oregano
- Salt and pepper to taste

Instructions:

For the Calzones:

1. Preheat your oven to 425°F (220°C). Line a baking sheet with parchment paper.
2. Divide the pizza dough into 8 equal portions. Roll each portion into a ball.
3. On a lightly floured surface, roll out each dough ball into a circle, about 6 inches in diameter.
4. In a mixing bowl, combine the ricotta cheese, mozzarella cheese, Parmesan cheese, chopped spinach, garlic powder, dried oregano, salt, and pepper. Mix until well combined.
5. Spoon a portion of the cheese and spinach mixture onto one half of each dough circle, leaving a border around the edges.
6. Fold the other half of the dough over the filling to create a half-moon shape. Press the edges firmly to seal, then crimp with a fork to secure.
7. Transfer the calzones to the prepared baking sheet. Brush the tops with olive oil.
8. Bake in the preheated oven for 15-20 minutes, or until the calzones are golden brown and crisp.
9. Remove from the oven and let them cool slightly before serving.

For the Marinara Dipping Sauce:

1. In a saucepan, heat olive oil over medium heat. Add minced garlic and sauté until fragrant, about 1 minute.
2. Stir in the crushed tomatoes, dried basil, dried oregano, salt, and pepper. Bring to a simmer.
3. Reduce the heat to low and let the sauce simmer for about 10 minutes, stirring occasionally, to allow the flavors to meld together.
4. Remove from heat and let the marinara sauce cool slightly before serving alongside the mini calzones.

Serve the mini calzones with the marinara dipping sauce on the side for a delicious appetizer or snack that's sure to please everyone!

Grilled Prosciutto-Wrapped Shrimp

Ingredients:

- 16 large shrimp, peeled and deveined, tails left on
- 8 slices prosciutto, sliced in half lengthwise
- Olive oil, for brushing
- Salt and black pepper, to taste
- Lemon wedges, for serving

Instructions:

1. Preheat your grill to medium-high heat.
2. Season the shrimp with salt and black pepper.
3. Wrap each shrimp with a half-slice of prosciutto, starting from the tail and wrapping towards the head. Secure the prosciutto with a toothpick if needed.
4. Brush the prosciutto-wrapped shrimp lightly with olive oil to prevent sticking on the grill.
5. Place the shrimp on the preheated grill and cook for 2-3 minutes per side, or until the shrimp are pink and opaque and the prosciutto is crispy.
6. Remove the shrimp from the grill and let them cool slightly before serving.
7. Serve the grilled prosciutto-wrapped shrimp with lemon wedges on the side for squeezing over the top.

Enjoy these flavorful and elegant grilled prosciutto-wrapped shrimp as an appetizer or main dish at your next gathering or barbecue!

Italian Herb and Cheese Pull-Apart Bread

Ingredients:

- 1 loaf of Italian bread or French baguette
- ½ cup unsalted butter, melted
- 2 cloves garlic, minced
- 2 tablespoons chopped fresh parsley
- 1 tablespoon chopped fresh basil
- 1 tablespoon chopped fresh oregano
- 1 cup shredded mozzarella cheese
- ½ cup shredded Parmesan cheese
- Salt and pepper, to taste

Instructions:

1. Preheat your oven to 375°F (190°C). Line a baking sheet with parchment paper.
2. Using a serrated knife, make diagonal cuts into the loaf of bread, spacing them about 1 inch apart and being careful not to cut all the way through the bottom crust.
3. In a small bowl, mix together the melted butter, minced garlic, chopped parsley, basil, and oregano.
4. Gently separate the bread slices and brush the herb butter mixture generously between each slice, making sure to get the butter into the cuts.
5. Stuff the shredded mozzarella cheese and Parmesan cheese between the slices, distributing evenly.
6. Season the top of the bread with a sprinkle of salt and pepper, if desired.
7. Wrap the loaf of bread in aluminum foil, leaving the top partially open to allow steam to escape.
8. Place the bread on the prepared baking sheet and bake in the preheated oven for 15-20 minutes, or until the cheese is melted and bubbly and the bread is golden brown.
9. Remove the bread from the oven and let it cool for a few minutes before serving.
10. Serve the Italian herb and cheese pull-apart bread warm, allowing everyone to pull off individual pieces.

Enjoy the irresistible combination of savory herbs and gooey cheese in this delicious pull-apart bread! It's perfect for serving as an appetizer, snack, or side dish.

Sautéed Garlic Butter Shrimp

Ingredients:

- 1 pound large shrimp, peeled and deveined
- 4 tablespoons unsalted butter
- 4 cloves garlic, minced
- 1 tablespoon olive oil
- 1 tablespoon fresh lemon juice
- 1 tablespoon chopped fresh parsley
- Salt and black pepper, to taste
- Lemon wedges, for serving
- Cooked pasta, rice, or crusty bread, for serving (optional)

Instructions:

1. Pat the shrimp dry with paper towels and season them with salt and black pepper to taste.
2. In a large skillet, heat the olive oil and 2 tablespoons of butter over medium-high heat until the butter is melted and foaming.
3. Add the minced garlic to the skillet and sauté for about 30 seconds, or until fragrant.
4. Add the seasoned shrimp to the skillet in a single layer, making sure not to overcrowd the pan. Cook the shrimp for 1-2 minutes on each side, or until they are pink and opaque.
5. Once the shrimp are cooked through, add the remaining 2 tablespoons of butter to the skillet, along with the fresh lemon juice and chopped parsley. Toss everything together until the shrimp are evenly coated in the garlic butter sauce and the butter is melted.
6. Remove the skillet from the heat and transfer the sautéed garlic butter shrimp to a serving platter.
7. Serve the shrimp immediately, garnished with additional chopped parsley and lemon wedges on the side.
8. You can serve the sautéed garlic butter shrimp on its own as an appetizer, or as a main course with cooked pasta, rice, or crusty bread on the side to soak up the delicious sauce.

Enjoy this simple and flavorful sautéed garlic butter shrimp recipe! It's sure to be a hit with seafood lovers.

Mediterranean Stuffed Mini Peppers

Ingredients:

- 12-16 mini bell peppers, assorted colors
- 1 cup cooked quinoa or couscous
- 1 cup cherry tomatoes, diced
- ½ cup cucumber, diced
- ½ cup Kalamata olives, chopped
- ¼ cup red onion, finely chopped
- ¼ cup crumbled feta cheese
- 2 tablespoons fresh parsley, chopped
- 2 tablespoons fresh lemon juice
- 2 tablespoons extra virgin olive oil
- 1 teaspoon dried oregano
- Salt and black pepper, to taste

Instructions:

1. Preheat your oven to 375°F (190°C). Line a baking sheet with parchment paper.
2. Cut the tops off the mini bell peppers and remove the seeds and membranes. Set aside.
3. In a large mixing bowl, combine the cooked quinoa or couscous, diced cherry tomatoes, diced cucumber, chopped Kalamata olives, finely chopped red onion, crumbled feta cheese, chopped parsley, fresh lemon juice, extra virgin olive oil, dried oregano, salt, and black pepper. Mix until well combined.
4. Stuff each mini bell pepper with the quinoa or couscous mixture, pressing down gently to pack the filling.
5. Place the stuffed mini peppers on the prepared baking sheet.
6. Bake in the preheated oven for 15-20 minutes, or until the peppers are tender and the filling is heated through.
7. Remove from the oven and let the stuffed mini peppers cool slightly before serving.
8. Serve the Mediterranean stuffed mini peppers warm or at room temperature as a flavorful appetizer or side dish.

Enjoy these Mediterranean stuffed mini peppers as a vibrant and tasty addition to your next meal or gathering! They're packed with wholesome ingredients and make for a delightful bite.

Fried Mozzarella and Tomato Bites

Ingredients:

- Fresh mozzarella cheese, sliced into bite-sized pieces
- Ripe tomatoes, sliced into rounds
- All-purpose flour
- Eggs, beaten
- Bread crumbs (you can use seasoned or plain)
- Salt and pepper to taste
- Vegetable oil for frying
- Marinara sauce for dipping (optional)

Instructions:

1. Prepare the Ingredients:
    - Slice the fresh mozzarella into bite-sized pieces.
    - Slice the tomatoes into rounds, ensuring they are not too thick.
2. Coat the Mozzarella and Tomatoes:
    - Set up three shallow bowls. Fill one with all-purpose flour, one with beaten eggs, and the third one with bread crumbs.
    - Season the bread crumbs with salt and pepper to taste.
    - Dip each mozzarella slice into the flour, shaking off any excess.
    - Next, dip the floured mozzarella slice into the beaten egg, ensuring it's coated evenly.
    - Finally, coat the mozzarella in the seasoned bread crumbs, pressing gently to adhere. Repeat this process for all mozzarella pieces.
    - Repeat the same process for the tomato slices, coating them in flour, egg, and breadcrumbs.
3. Fry the Mozzarella and Tomatoes:
    - Heat vegetable oil in a frying pan over medium heat.
    - Once the oil is hot, carefully add the coated mozzarella and tomato slices in batches, ensuring not to overcrowd the pan.
    - Fry until golden brown and crispy, turning once to ensure even cooking, about 2-3 minutes per side.
    - Once cooked, remove the fried mozzarella and tomato bites from the oil and place them on a plate lined with paper towels to drain excess oil.
4. Serve:
    - Arrange the fried mozzarella and tomato bites on a serving platter.
    - Serve them hot with marinara sauce for dipping, if desired.
    - Enjoy your delicious Fried Mozzarella and Tomato Bites as a tasty appetizer or snack!

Feel free to adjust the seasoning according to your taste preferences, and enjoy these crispy, cheesy bites!